I0334806

BACKLASH
PRESS

A pioneering publishing house dedicated to creating intelligent, vivid books.

Established to inform, educate, entertain and provoke.

Journal One

A Backlash Book
First published 2015
Reprinted 2024

backlashpress.com
ISBN: 978-1-0686972-3-4

Designer:
The Scrutineer, Rachael Adams.
Fonts: Baskerville, Bree serif.
Printed and bound by IngramSpark.

Contents

Editor: Gret Heffernan. A poetry collection to be read as a continuous story inside a communal narrative.

Erica Bernheim

You Who Seek Smart Things

The world begins and ends here:
the tour guide admits he has yet
to visit the places in front of which
now we stand. Hello, danger! Hello,
bones! You may be quite ugly,
but you are not really here. Sometimes
hot water flows from a cold faucet.
Please remember to realize how the
things you love can still disappear.

Leonard Gontarek

Field

1

There is a line that is invisible,
flecked with silver, that goes
through everything.
There is a map at the back
of this book, in pencil, with roads
marked one through *seven*.

When some time has passed,
the roar is a distant waterfall.
The flowers that come from the ground
are purple and yellow,
are red, with scent of anise and death.
I don't remember what it is a map of anymore.

I wish the birds were returning, reversing the past.
We can't get our bearings, sweet truck back-up *beep*.

2

The heart
breaks like a paperweight.

Rewind and it restores.
Broken, always ends up,

eventually, broken.
Still. What, still?

I want to read the paper
in the sleeping man's hand. I can't

pry open. I imagine
the story in the curled pages.

I walk into a field of fragile things,
abide, descend.

Mary Gurr

Marriage

That morning the sea had been diamond blue,
bright metal blue and then bone-meal green;
and after the sky had lightened from thick, mercurial
blue-whale blue, darker than the sea, to pale infinity,
a fishing trawler, long and dark like a black bullet
submarine, gun-black man-of-war, a monster,
pushed its way sedately west to east towards
the rising sun: for five minutes nothing else moved,
nothing obvious, and then a small silver car, its lights
still on, hummed slowly up the coast road, accelerated
round the bend, dropped to a lower tone
and disappeared. This marked the beginning of the end
of the quiet period, between the dawn chorus
and the day – which that morning lasted
an hour and twenty minutes – before the sky,
the sea and all the other silver cars were joined
together in holy grey, to be forever cloudy.

Charles Clifford Brooks III

The Original Title Failed Me

I may lie to my heart,
but my heart never lies to me.

You've Found Another Lover
(I've Lost Another Friend)
-Ben Harper & Charlie Musslewhite

I.

What's most uncommon
is your skin. The moment I brush it,
hold it close to my cheek,
the smooth calm of it
keeps me in stasis
when the world is usually
a blur. The entire of you has severe lines,
but not one hard edge.

This short drive to you
gives me the gap autos often provide
where I recollect how exotic you seemed
a week ago,
last night,
even

now
I think about
how your bangs frame
a profile Jane Austen
would describe
as beautiful and brave.

You are foreign to me.
I didn't know then, little more now,
how to let what flows
deepest in me,
come loose to you. The wrenches for reaching
so far have been lost over the years.
Long in the tooth,
bitter feels frighteningly
permanent.

...

You see, I don't have a lexicon,
a pliable language
to let you know
you're like snow in June.

We are suspicious things to a species
stuck in neutral.

We are not them, sweet pea.
One minute –
the cigarette, the excuse to steal a hug;
in those scant seconds
we are scarcely seen
in this busy cosmos.

Before dinner,
Jeff Buckley reminds us
to have faith.
I realize the bedroom is our church.
A pearl necklace drapes
around your young neck.
That perfume is brand new,
and twists its way up
into my sense of decency.

II.

While rambling around Rome with you
I could hear
the college nearby I once enjoyed,
and the complicity between us.
Sunshine through a window
lights up the gold flecks
in your green eyes.

Traffic isn't creeping,
or tragic
in this hour slender in dissatisfaction,
and full of good feeling.
You, me – it is different.

III.

Untimely fireworks explode
in October, this evening,
due to a July
too wet to enjoy them.
We watch the wild display
and deem ourselves weird,
but we're
that perfect, complimentary
kind of weird
where the heart
is wholly unhindered.

We are similar,
but not mathematically exact.
From that wellspring has
come our only poisonous discussions.
This is no complaint,
more a point of interest.

How do you interpret it?

You said:
I wish you'd allow yourself
time away from
the galaxy in your head,
and more time
in the stars with me.

Erica Bernheim

Wednesday

At night we bloom this vast world of indifference.
What we have been warned of returns, one foot
revealed is one foot lost. We too must end. Come
to this table naked but for your silent pinched shoulders.

It is easier to do it this way: why plan the end to these days
when it's better than staying to watch you attach,
picking up perpetual errands, any telephone, awaiting
the flutter of so many hairs falling in circles, the crash

of the leg, grounded and painless. Your game face
has shattered me. Your obtuse kindness has bored
into me, made of me a snail, stuck in sawdust, vapor
ignorant of its own rise to form echoes. If it has to end,

this day too ends with the knowledge of my love post-
meridian. I swear it shall be the last. How many times
in a day can I look to your notes, ask questions that are
not at all what I mean. Devour and consume, as though

you knew why from this love, nothing keeps me but you.

Leonard Gontarek

Gleamed

1

They fished the sky.
The rocks gleamed, the rocks disappeared. Clearly they saw this.
They continued drying their hands after they were dry.
We all do this. In one way

or another, we always do this.
They thought footprints made sense, to a point.
Fingerprints, less so. They planted in fall,
they planted in spring, they planted in summer.

They bundled their souls in layers of clothes.
They brought jars of ants, unless they forgot them.
They brought cold chicken, they brought sherbet. You got to love them for that.
They were alone, small stacks of firewood.

2

It wasn't like a dream.
The lights moved and settled.
Rain continued to fall.
No one was hurt.

How you define *hurt* depends on much.
The egg of the world we carried
broke. The day was now
in another summer.

Those we knew in that
car were safe.
The fireflies
above the lawn had begun to sink.

Could we have known, we would have stayed home always,
the soul broken in four equal parts.

God

1

I've got no pull with God.
Just because you're paranoid, doesn't mean someone isn't following you.
The woods are frightened of you and withdraws its beauty.

The poem is a realism-and-joy delivery system.
Why has he come? To demystify and fumigate the American Poem, the man at the door tells me.
I've got no pull with God.

I'm a nutcase from the nuthouse driving like crazy around the house.
Little monsters on the living room floor, playing with super heroes.
The woods are frightened of you and withdraws its beauty.

I write to you no longer of visions I have, but ones I remember.
The moon, big and gold in the field, locks in for good.
I've got no pull with God.

I have my skeleton costume on inside, in case.
Food smells, at evening, bird sounds.
The woods are frightened of you and withdraws its beauty.
Sure there will be a last fling and a moments of its old self,

but I just feel sorry now for winter.
I've got no pull with God.
The woods are frightened of you and withdraws its beauty.

2

You can't go anywhere again.
I fell down, I fell down in one day.
Autumn, are you breaking up with me?

The hearse was filled with oranges.
At one point, the hearse was filled with oranges.
You can't go home again, you can't go anywhere again.

I wouldn't miss it.
Scarlet and orange, the forests rusting.
Are you breaking up with me?

There are many reasons.
Autumn, for example.
You can't go anywhere again, you can't go home.

Can a bridge be fashioned?
From there to there?
Autumn, you are breaking up with me?

It is through the light that the soul gets past.
Drink left outside, overnight.
You can't go anywhere again?
Autumn, you are breaking up with me.

Connor Stratman

Photograph

On the hill, there's a shine
beyond you and me, beyond
some knowing of what's what.
The wind is a thing. It's like
a tie you can't tie right,
but it's a trickling feeling
in your fingers, a dryness
quenched by rain in the right
seasons. Like our faces, the
mountains are drawn with light.

Mary Gurr

At Ballycroy

The mountains wrap around you
in a great big hug, at least,
that's what I tell myself before
they threaten to engulf.

Close up in daylight there's
little to intimidate, just the usual
big, bosomy aunties,
the ones who stayed at home.

In the blind night you almost
hear their gentle snoring,
slumped together,
ten in a bed.

To pass you have to drive
round or take your life in hand,
strike out on foot, negotiate rock,
bog, holes, fog, the dark.

Like sisters, more holds them
than parts them. I wind the window down,
let my fingers trace their blurry contours,

consider: should I get out?

But I don't, they might unwittingly
lash out in sleep,
revive old nightmares,
wake up hungry.

Leonard Gontarek

North Calais Elegies

1

I long to speak the language my poems are in.
I long to do more than order them & greet you.

I long to do more than to wake in the arms of dark.
Loons & a boat loose in the lake like meaning.

Blessed are those who live close to the dead.
A family plot just over the rise.

Blessed are the trees, silver on one side,
dark on the other.

Praise my mother going under the knife.
Praise the years of the rustle & *hiss* of Pall Malls.

Praise the waiting room, praise leafing through a *New Yorker*.
Praise the doctor, it was hours before he lied to us,

told us the cancer wasn't everywhere.

Already the leaves drift.
The surf of cars on Pine Street.

I stand as far in the corner of the yard as I can.
Shadows begin to unspool.

Five o'clock at the end of the garden. Gold snow among snow.
I forget my key & use the hidden key.

I climb over the gate.
There are shadows, shadows.

Blessed are those who have come before me,
ducked under the dark.

The moon slides behind a cloud, darkens the edges.
Blessed are my neighbors who like to talk outdoors.

The lawn chairs creak.
Blessed are my neighbors who lift the King of Beers from a chest of diamonds.

Blessed are insects & tree frogs who own the night world.
In impaired, incandescent language, they argue the point.

Three teenagers stare into the open hood of a car.
Better not tell them they resemble three grown men standing over a front

garden,

offering bullet-points of mocking, but good-natured advice.
The owner makes mental note, because in the end,

the information is useful & he has to admit, witty
& each of them is confused & a little sad,

& none of them want to see the hydrangea die.

Blessed is the dog barking at nothing, we are fairly certain.
It became summer overnight.

Blessed is the source of the mysterious we can't locate.
Once I wasn't. Then I was. Now I ain't again.

Blessed are the fresh, green sheets of the trees. Blessed is laundry
twirling in a dryer.
The source of the mysterious we can't locate.

The planes go over the world. Blessed are the shadows.
Blessed are the white & purple tulips. They have passed. We must
replace them.

Autumn. I believe it is the exact turning point, but it is probably not.
Praise the bird that calls out & stops.

Praise the subway under the house, or the washer in spin cycle.
I've never seen, I believe, the trees this green, now that they are leaving
me.

Praise the flickering black lacquer & raw jade.
Praise the painting, which is not finished, in which peasants are baling
twilight.

Blessed is the shadow that used to pass over. Now goes right through us.

Blessed are the trees on fire, but beautiful, in October.
Later, without leaves, in snowdrifts of gray light, late in the day,

Praise my father who asked to be buried in the backyard.
Praise the neighbors, Cecilia & Joe, for instance,

who will inquire about the racket & the terrific mound of dirt,
some of which rattled into their backyard.

How could we tell them this was *beauty*, this was *legend*,
standing there like a bunch of teenaged drunks around a car plowed into
a pole?

2

Praise Cecilia & Joe who see a grown man mowing & weeping.

Connor Stratman

Screen(s)

Nothing clarifies the backdrop: *it* or *that*
and *this*. Powerless crumbles the person

trolling in a folding garden, rich growth
and failed seedlings is this: a circle. Not

its measurements but its tact, its "feeling."
Even our sins don't count against it: void.

A payment unmakeable, a sting ungiven.
Living in the building, carving imperfect

shapes, assumed along a cracking line, I,
this some*thing*, is a flick of the red palms.

Solidifying Air

is entangled with trapped dreams
where one thing becomes another
like a pine into a brontosaurus
or a city into a birdclaw
Lilywhite becoming sand
are the sheets now in good time
this is the corner you used to meet
the man and his dog
you fed each other and shared
tobacco scraps through
the afternoon of torrents

Mary Gurr

Lauren Bacall's Tee-shirt

Or Betty to her friends, like my friend Carole
dresser to Bacall, owner of the tee-shirt
before it passed to me: pale green, the same
mutton-fat jade as Elizabeth Bishop's wind-blown

ocean in 'The End of March', flecked with tiny
Swinging London oval mirrors; hard to imagine
Lauren '*put your lips together and blow*' Bacall clad in
1960s hippy chic, that what had touched her breasts

touched mine. O those good old 1960s, age of cults
when youth became its own denomination, turned
unto itself, dressed and loved itself, loved and sometimes
killed itself, loved and killed others, sometimes.

A relic of the ghost of '69, it stretched
across my braless breasts, my pets, those youthful
up-thrust wonders, little mirrors
twinkling at the nipple ends.

Another actor, Terry, used to stare at them,
pretend to see himself reflected, dazzled
by the frankness of their freedom, let his trembling
fingers brush them by mistake.

It’s possible she never wore it, could have
tried it on for size, for a laugh, to spend a moment
in another life, another sort of acting, the kind
we do ourselves in real-life.

She might have bought it as a gift but found it
too difficult to give, or in error, or a ruse
to break into a ten pound note, extravagant
change for the cigarette machine.

John Dorsey

Drunk John

gave me $7 and a cigar snip
for my 25th birthday
the morning his girlfriend
kicked him out
of their spruce street apartment.

the year before
i'd watched as she passed him
love notes in hindi
across the bar
while he listened
to iggy pop
on the jukebox
as it rained outside.

i could swear he was crying
when he sang happy birthday
under the busted street light.

Kyle Hemmings

Post-apocalyptic Fable #1

In the heavy ozone cast
of breathlessness
I kneel next to the girl
I shot by the abandoned
railway. I had mistaken
her for a far-sighted sniper,
now a mercenary leaking out
abstract patterns of life in red ink.
The same color of my blood.
Perhaps, under torture,
the two of us would never give
the other away. We'd smear
feces over the prison walls.
I swear.
In the drizzle of not-quite-rain,
I will sleep inside her,
before she turns to stone,
before I begin to feel
not quite alive.

John Dorsey

Sarah

had meth teeth
& an ass that hadn't quit
since just after vietnam.

she had barely finished the 10th grade
and was as good a therapist
as anyone with an ivy league degree
and she could pour a drink

like the virgin mary.

Creepy Steve

looked like an albino
on heroin.

he would start the day
with a boilermaker
before launching into stories
about how the government
was paying outer space aliens
to abduct nazi war criminals.

half way through he'd fall asleep.

he told me that if i ever needed
a job in argentina
to just let him know.

Kyle Hemmings

Post-apocalyptic Fable #2

We uncovered the burnt bodies
from the latest plutonium-perfect blast.
The bodies belonging to *them*
rose like new truths,
or perhaps old ones redefining
parameters. It now hurt to breathe.
We dropped to our knees.
Some attempted to fornicate with stones
as if their entire lives were built on lies.
Some of us took out our razor-sharp
army knives & neutered ourselves.
We understood that our future babies
would be missing a limb & a wing.

John Dorsey

Mary Ellen

wore an eye patch
and hung paintings on the wall
just above my barstool.

she noticed the little things
like the moon hung crooked
on your lips

and all of the little ghosts
in our eyes.

Jessica

taught french poetry
to the bridge and tunnel crowd
sipped warm beer
& fingered herself to bukowski
in the bathroom

she said
she got moist
at the sight of a tool belt

the only blue collar
thing about her

was her credit score.

Kyle Hemmings

Post-apocalyptic Fable #3

As a civilian casualty
she was missing an eye
& two fingers
trained on white piano keys.
She secluded herself in
a small cottage upon a hill
shaped like a door knob, locked.
When we questioned her
about aiding & abetting the enemy,
she blinked twice with her good eye.
Her speech was garbled.
Her breath was fetid & her teeth were green.
The moldy carpet began to form clumps.
Then, a thousand eyes rose from the floor,
began to interrogate us.

John Dorsey

Gary

christina and i watched gary
sing ac/dc covers
the first time we held hands.

she sat sipping a corona
& i told her
that i wasn't drinking anymore
that when looked into her eyes

i felt drunk
without having to run up a tab
that ours was a love

done dirt cheap.

Patrick Herron

<<<1000: squirrel suicides>>>

it was the age of the squirrel suicides   trees were giving up but
they could not run   the squirrels became apprehensive of storing
nuts for the winter   they were running out of nuts   they were
running nuts into the streets   jumping off the highest limbs   to
the pavement   the sound of nuts cracking all day   crack
crack crack   get cracking   and then fewer and fewer   the
agonies of the fluctuations of numbers   are they counting the trees
suggested that the squirrels go elsewhere after a long-standing contract
between flora and fauna   I'd like to see a timelapse image sequence
of untended pavement   by photography standards the demise of
pavement would be slow maybe   one hundred years   I am not
that old how about you   at what age will you cease to be lucky to
be alive   some want something else by the end   something other
just like the earth   how fast the roads go   by the something
else I mean by the end of taking pictures of pavement over a century
compared to the stone unprocessed by man   it's always moving but
it does so slowly   it seems to stick around as the pavement goes the
way of the squirrel   the nuts   the trees   humanity   I want
to pave my soul and take pictures of it to see if it is moving while the
squirrels are being run over on the top   can it be counted   it I
mean   these progression algorithms lack any sense of time   that
is to say they lack any sense of place   we gather to say we have
paused to be here   to be together   otherwise we are timeless and
nowhere and I'm not sure how that can be any comfort   not unless

you are ready to die   and die unsentimentally   die unmentally
not me   not I   I am not down with the squirrels   by the
Ashbery bridge I saw a squirrel the color of chocolate   it sat next to
me eating a nut   our fields met   this was before the age of squirrel
suicides   we paused   or was it the beginning   when was it that
where was it began to mean   when was it if we are to get counting we
must get cracking

<<<1010: decompression>>>

getting tired of the intervals   the sea scaped   chopped into
language moves   a squared be squared is sea squared   alpha
wolves organize the other members and lead cooperative hunts for
large species   the milieu is hardly species specific   I have
reasons but no backdrop for a quest I am not on Lunar the Blue Star
and haven't heard of it no   I am going to the moon glued to the
television dreaming of precision-guidance not werewolved but more
like sea-monkeyed   we live because of the latencies where else
would a robot steering guidance system inhabit the space forming a
cause and forming a response the same response is this an overlapping
in-flight alignment through strapdown algorithms unupholstered and
silvery tasting like batteries strangely   the same dragons keep arising
there is a line here somewhere   I suffer great anxiety in the face of
long lines and stay away from them flee from them a solitary milieu
repeated aperiodically yet fragrant   his cioppino was great holy
Toldeo but a little more tomato in our broth   how close do you live
to the sea a nice dish to save up for when there's the taste of salt marsh
riding the wind coursing through the slight gap between your lips like
a breath that consumes all digesting lovingly and myriad   flashing
forward to buck rogers and no one does it better   it is not sufficient
simply to make the building blocks   one must also worry about the
structure and chemistry of their surfaces and how they will interact
one with another or with a matrix in which they are embedded a very
wide range of diverse synthesis and assembly strategies being employed

in nanostructuring all the way from fundamental biological methods for
selfassembling for making clusters or then dispersing them or bringing
them together in consolidated forms   each media regime and each
system of signification projects a specific configuration of the subject and
a horizon of agency as a consequence of its normal operation projecting
a virtual user   mirrored simulating and what isn't the it that isn't isn't
easy to find   if I have I've forgotten I'm too busy being reassembled
who's asking about who's making the specific too specific for well
just   specific   signage with the fences that embed them vegetal and
differential   what it is is the equating is the amplifying sound invisible
but all things are touched eventually   it's nothing to do with what I
mean   her one when she was making americans that was one alright
one is not in the speaking so much as in the conversation   it's the one
not in there   it's here and liliputian fried to a golden   asking you
about your left hand right now is a strange thing to ask and where's the
conversation in this   so tired I wonder should I   justified true belief
in what you might put around what you converse what's left out of it
really right beside it around it   to ask how might a piano evolve given
a choice of where it wants to assemble itself into a sense   homunculi
gone wild   an opportunistic   this hairy little critter is probably
oblivious to the fact that while it feasts on an acorn it and its fellow
squirrels are overrunning the university   this isn't significant find me
something signifying and another mirror only another mirror another
ghost   it has always been there whether scaped or pythagorean or
humble portmanteau of the speaking and eating   the congruencies
are amplifying resonantly in three flavor neutrinos that have been released

into the ring   and as I have said before these algorithms lack any sense of time   the time is where the algorithm is not   that thing where it isn't   the blood that fills our mouths and oh my god how I love you one will cut the names loose Gertrude   how is even one an effect   a worldwide run on the supply of optimistic geneticists some are against genes   if you want you can go back to the world of progress   what exactly is this ghost this simulation machine right here is making   manchine summarization execution transitional or complete

<<<1011: the marriage of earth and dearth>>>

the Higgs boson in many religions spiritual traditions and philosophies
is the spiritual and eternal part of a living being   the soul is a
massive   the way things repeat   scalar elementary particle
predicted   commonly held to be separable   in existence from the
body as distinct   from the physical part   to exist by the Standard
Model   specifically the way bad events erect a pair of rubber walls
send you bounding off them like a ball   to consist of a human's
consciousness and personality   the Higgs boson is believed   it is
typically thought   to live on after the person's physical death   back
and forth the oscillation not dampening but gaining   nature the soul
is the only Standard Model particle   and sometimes inanimate objects
are said to   and can   have Higgs bosons a belief known as animism
that has not yet been observed   interchangeably although the
former may be   between the massless photon which mediates
electromagnetism and the massive W and Z spirits which mediate the
weak   maybe I might   maybe not   synonymously   closely to
metaphysics   in some cultures non-human living things   that God
creates Higgs bosons   and religion   force   it makes me sick in
my stomach   and some religions posit   in particle physics at present
there   are no known fundamental scalar particles in   transcendent
aspect of a person than the latter   experimental detection of the soul
would help   explain the origin of mass in the   stuck on repeat
although 'psyche' has relatively more physical connotations   i've never
arrived   be synonymous with the spirit mind or self   between

winning and losing more losing than winning simply because the losing sticks   whereas ‘Higgs boson’ is connected more   the soul would explain the difference   the terms ‘Higgs boson’ and ‘psyche’ can also be treated   universe more specifically   viewed as a more worldly and less   the terms Higgs boson and spirit are often used an integral and pervasive component of the material world   if the soul exists it is   if the soul exists it is   empires lions and wolves fire in sunlight   withdraw what is half-given   scatter hording or larder   while they last

<<<embedded 1100: apples and onions>>>

apples and onions and violins and pesticides   and when viewing from
a bridge the horizon is only half-constructed   what knife various apes
select for gorging is technically determined   various timbres of icy
water sing across the bowed fibers of our skulls   their smell of spray
as the roaches as they are now called the worthless are swept down into
the legs running on the air between nature and nurture and someone's
just learning how to count them the forty-seven percent the ninety nine
my beautiful son he is learning as he goes please don't push him off   if
he is falling I pray let his curls hear the quartet the helicopters need trust
between them first before they can make music   how about our sweet
beginnings and chopped vegetable tears plucked from soil to lighten
the load the roman road yes it's a load we load to unload and unload to
load   it's a logic   we share it with our peelings   the lacrimal
bone is absent from amphibians or maybe it's just tardy or wants nothing
to do with tears at all   maybe it's trying to get out of the water or
maybe any more would be an unsophisticated superfluity   and you are
similarly disinclined to travel beyond the elegant sufficiency yet you made
it this far and so let's exchange gratitudes they sure scissor paper platitudes
and stony attitudes   what to say that is not desired here is that it's not
the bullet that kills you it's the hole it's of an infinite dimension   but
when I say I care about you I mean that I desire the chance to elaborate
and that is to say that I hope that you have not had to learn that it's the
hollow that's the only part that doesn't hurt   what hurts is what can
be counted   so I wonder is emptiness employed or unemployed how

are we to count that   so I wonder is love conflation or expansion
how are we to feel our way through the choppers and make horizons
"you're taut like a thriller but how are you organized?" the rock asks the river

BACKLASH

PRESS

www.ingramcontent.com/pod-product-compliance
Lightning Source LLC
Chambersburg PA
CBHW030458010526
44118CB00011B/1003